KU-107-752

Text Structures

Life Cycle of a Leopard

A Sequence and Order Text

Phillip Simpson

Raintree

Raintree is an imprint of Capstone Global Library Limited, a company incorporated in England and Wales having its registered office at 7 Pilgrim Street, London, EC4V 6LB – Registered company number: 6695582

www.raintreepublishers.co.uk
myorders@raintreepublishers.co.uk

Text © Capstone Global Library Limited 2015
First published in hardback in 2014
The moral rights of the proprietor have been asserted.

All rights reserved. No part of this publication may be reproduced in any form or by any means (including photocopying or storing it in any medium by electronic means and whether or not transiently or incidentally to some other use of this publication) without the written permission of the copyright owner, except in accordance with the provisions of the Copyright, Designs, and Patents Act 1988 or under the terms of a licence issued by the Copyright Licensing Agency, Saffron House, 6–10 Kirby Street, London EC1N 8TS (www.cla.co.uk). Applications for the copyright owner's written permission should be addressed to the publisher.

Edited by Diyan Leake and Kathryn Clay
Designed by Steve Mead
Picture research by Tracy Cummins
Production by Helen McCreath
Originated by Capstone Global Library Ltd
Printed and bound in China by Leo Paper Group

ISBN 978 1 406 28353 2
18 17 16 15 14
10 9 8 7 6 5 4 3 2 1

British Library Cataloguing in Publication Data
A full catalogue record for this book is available from the British Library.

Acknowledgements
We would like to thank the following for permission to reproduce photographs: Corbis: © Gallo Images, 17, © Nigel Pavitt/JAI, 12, 8 top right, © Richard Du Toit/Minden Pictures, 16; Getty Images: Roy Toft / National Geographic, 19; Naturepl.com: © Andy Rouse, 27, 14, 15, 21, 24, © Christophe Courteau, 9, © Denis-Huot, 20, © Pete Oxford, 10, © RICHARD DU TOIT, 13, © Sergey Gorshkov, 23, © T.J. RICH, 5; Shutterstock: creativex, 8 bottom right, 18, Dave Pusey, 4, 11, davemhuntphotography, 25, Jakub Krechowicz, 29 (notebook), Ohishiapply, 28, Papa Bravo, 26, Sarah Cheriton-Jones, 6, Sharon Haeger, 7, 8 top left, Stu Porter, 8 bottom left, urfin, 29 (pen), wildpix, 22.

Cover photograph reproduced with permission of Naturepl.com, © Anup Shah.

Artistic effects
Shutterstock: Livijus Raubickas, Olga Kovalenko, Peshkova, Roman Sotola, Sarah Cheriton-Jones

Every effort has been made to contact copyright holders of material reproduced in this book. Any omissions will be rectified in subsequent printings if notice is given to the publisher.

All the Internet addresses (URLs) given in this book were valid at the time of going to press. However, due to the dynamic nature of the Internet, some addresses may have changed, or sites may have changed or ceased to exist since publication. While the author and publisher regret any inconvenience this may cause readers, no responsibility for any such changes can be accepted by either the author or the publisher.

Contents

The text in this book has been organized using the sequence and order text structure. The sequence and order text structure describes things in a sequence from beginning to end. To find out more about writing using this text structure, see page 28.

Some words are shown in bold, **like this**. You can find out what they mean by looking in the glossary.

What is a leopard?

The leopard is a member of a group of animals known as "big cats". The true big cats include the leopard, lion, tiger and jaguar. The leopard can be found in some parts of Africa and Asia. It is listed as a near threatened species because of hunting and loss of **habitat**.

The leopard is the smallest of the true big cats.

The leopard is a **carnivore** and is **nocturnal**, hunting mostly at night. It prefers to hunt and live alone. Leopards are excellent climbers, spending much of their time in trees. To protect its **prey** from other animals, the leopard sometimes drags it high up into trees.

Leopards often carry their prey into trees.

What does a leopard look like?

A leopard has short, powerful legs and a large skull. The strong build helps leopards drag prey. The leopard has light-coloured fur with dark spots. Leopards with dark fur are sometimes called black panthers.

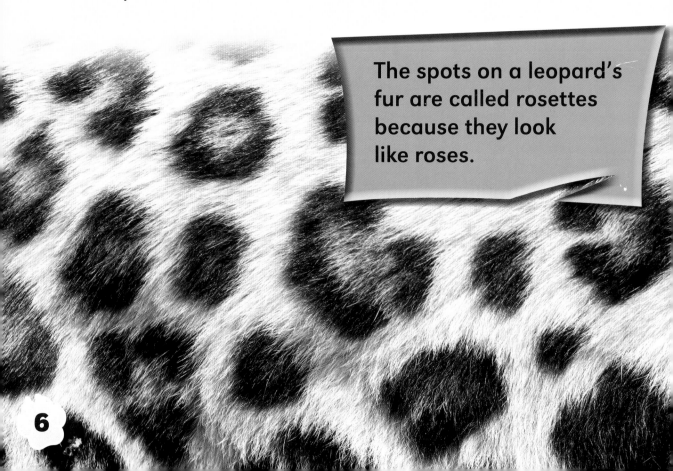

The spots on a leopard's fur are called rosettes because they look like roses.

The leopard uses its camouflage to sneak up on prey.

The leopard's fur provides excellent **camouflage**, allowing it to blend in with leaves, trees and grass. This makes the leopard a very successful **predator**. It can **ambush** its prey, which includes antelope, deer and pigs. The leopard is also able to run very fast, reaching speeds of 58 kilometres (36 miles) per hour.

What is a life cycle?

The **life cycle** of an animal is all the stages of its life from birth to death. The life cycle of each animal can range from weeks to many years. During a life cycle, an animal grows and changes. When the animal becomes an adult, it produces its own young. This is known as **reproduction**.

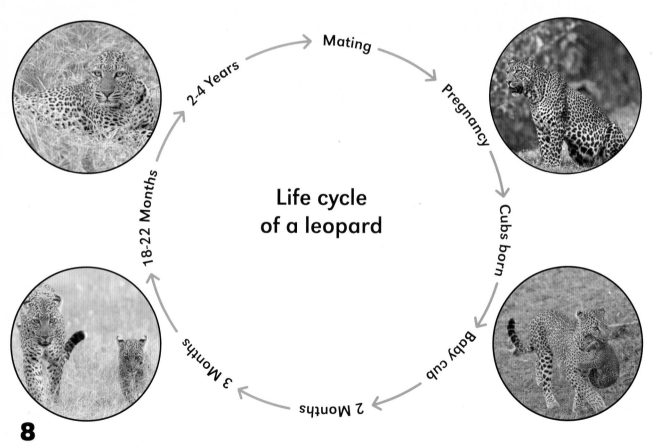

Life cycle
of a leopard

Mating

2-4 Years

Pregnancy

18-22 Months

Cubs born

3 Months

Baby cub

2 Months

Leopards, like humans, are mammals. Mammals have hair or fur, are warm-blooded and feed their young with milk. Almost all mammals give birth to live young. This means that their young are born from the mother's body instead of hatching from an egg like reptiles, fish and insects.

Young leopards feed on milk from their mother.

Mating and reproduction

Adult male and female leopards seek out each other and **mate**. Male and female leopards are rarely together except during the mating period. Mating can happen at any time of year.

Males and females avoid each other except during mating.

Male leopards prefer to live alone.

A female tells a male she is ready to mate by making a particular smell or sound. A male leopard will then make its way into the female's **territory**. The mating period lasts only a few days. As soon as it is over, the male returns to his own territory.

Gestation

The next stage is **gestation**. Gestation is the period of time that a female carries a baby inside her before it is ready to be born. For a leopard, the gestation time is about three months. During this time, the baby leopard grows and changes, getting ready for life outside its mother's body.

The gestation period for a leopard is about three months.

Young cubs are completely dependent on their mother.

A female leopard is able to have young when she is about two years old. She will keep mating with male leopards until she becomes pregnant. Once she has had her cubs, she will not be ready to mate again until after her cubs have left to find their own territories.

Newborn cubs

After gestation the **litter** is born. Leopards usually have two to three cubs in a litter. Sometimes the mother can have up to six cubs at one time. The cubs are born with their eyes closed, and they are unable to hear. Their fur looks very different from that of an adult, with spots that are barely visible.

No two leopards have the same spots. Each is unique, like fingerprints.

Walking is an important step in a leopard's life cycle.

Newborn leopards weigh about 0.45 to 0.9 kilograms (1 to 2 pounds). After about seven to 10 days, they will open their eyes. At about two weeks old, the cubs begin to walk.

Birth locations

After a female becomes pregnant, she begins to look for a **den** to give birth to her cubs. These dens are often found in a cave, bushes, rock pile or hollow tree. They are usually very difficult for other predators to find. She will often change a den's location in order to keep her cubs safe.

A den must be safe from predators.

Cubs must remain completely silent in their den or predators might find them.

Because the newborn cubs are completely helpless, the mother stays in the den for the first few days after the birth to care for her cubs. After this time, the mother must leave the den to hunt for food.

Caring for newborn cubs

The mother leopard licks the newborn cubs with her rough tongue. This helps to increase their blood circulation. She keeps them warm with her body and feeds them with her milk.

Leopards will carry cubs in their mouths.

The mother sometimes leaves the cubs unprotected for hours while she hunts.

Even when the mother goes out to hunt, she doesn't go far. She returns every few hours to feed her cubs. The cubs are hidden but unprotected. They know to keep silent even if they are hungry so they don't alert predators. For the next six to eight weeks, the cubs only play outside when their mother is around.

Three months old

The mother leopard begins to feed the cubs meat when they are six to eight weeks old. They are no longer completely dependent on their mother's milk. At three to four months, the cubs begin to follow their mother when she leaves the den. She still leaves them alone when she goes hunting.

The cubs follow the white tip on the bottom of their mother's tail.

Learning to hunt is one of the most important survival skills for a young leopard.

Because they cannot watch their mother hunt at this age, the cubs learn the skills for hunting by playing. The mother sometimes brings live animals such as baby antelopes back to the den. Doing so helps the cubs learn how to kill.

One year old

Once the cubs become strong enough to climb trees, the mother leads them further from their den. After one year, young leopards can hunt by themselves. They then begin to leave their mother for long periods of time and start to look for their own territories.

Learning to climb keeps a young leopard safe from predators.

Most young leopards are no match for hyenas.

Large prey such as pigs and baboons can often be too difficult for a young leopard to hunt by itself. If the mother does not help, the young leopard can sometimes be injured or killed. Young leopards are often robbed of their prey by larger predators, such as lions and hyenas. Fewer than half of all leopard cubs survive their first year.

Two years old

The young leopard stays with its mother until it is about 15 to 24 months. The mother often becomes unfriendly toward her cubs, forcing them to leave around this time. Most leopards at this age stay close to their mother's territory.

Young leopards stay with their mothers for two years.

When they are older and more confident, male leopards travel further away from their mother to find their own territory. Female leopards often live closer to their mothers than male leopards.

By age two, most leopards are fully independent. After this, their mother is ready to give birth to a new litter of cubs.

Leopards prefer to live on their own.

Lifespan

Before the age of three, leopards are not considered to be adults. If not injured or killed by other predators, leopards often live to between 12 and 15 years in the wild. In zoos, where they can live safely, leopards have been known to live more than 20 years.

Leopards do not live as long in the wild as they do in zoos.

Some leopards live more than 20 years in captivity.

The oldest leopard ever recorded was a female known as Bertie from Warsaw Zoo in Poland. She died in 2010 at the age of 24. The oldest male ever recorded was Bertie's companion, Cezar, also from Warsaw Zoo. He died at the age of 23.

Explanation of text structure

The information in this text is organized using the **sequence and order** text structure. In this text structure, information is organized by the order in which it happens. Words such as *first*, *next*, *before*, *lastly*, *after* and *then* are used to show the order in which things happen.

When they are a little older and more confident, male leopards travel further away from their mother to find their own territory. By age two, most young leopards are fully independent. After this, their mother is ready to give birth to a new litter of cubs.

Sequence and order signal words

Now you could try using the **sequence and order** text structure to write about the transformation of:
- a tadpole to a frog
- a seed to a sunflower
- grain to bread

Glossary

ambush a surprise attack

camouflage a natural colouring or body shape that allows an animal to blend in with its surroundings

carnivore an animal that eats meat

den a wild animal's home

gestation the time when a young animal is developing inside its mother; also known as pregnancy

habitat a natural home for an animal or plant

life cycle different stages of an organism's life

litter the number of babies born at one time

mate to come together to produce babies

nocturnal active at night

predator an animal that hunts and eats other animals

prey an animal that is hunted and eaten by other animals

reproduction the way in which an animal or plant produces one or more individuals similar to itself

territory the area an animal thinks of as its own

Find out more

Books

Can You Tell a Cheetah from a Leopard? (Animal Look-Alikes),
  Buffy Silverman (Lerner, 2012)

Face to Face with Leopards, Dereck and Beverly Joubert
  (National Geographic, 2010)

Snow Leopards (Big Cats), Dianna Dorisi-Winget
  (Capstone Press, 2012)

Websites

http://bigcatrescue.org/leopard-facts/
This website has lots of information about rescued leopards.

www.bbc.co.uk/nature/life/Leopard
See some some amazing videos of leopards on this website.

Index